TINY-
RANNOSAURUS

Nick Ward

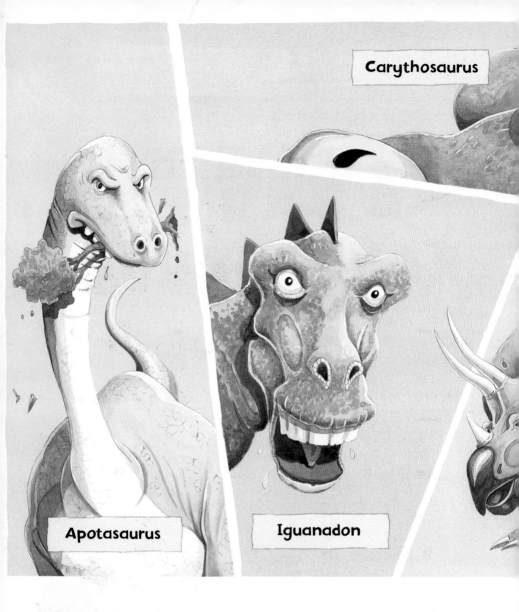

Many, many years ago, when the world was
a wild and dangerous place, when everywhere
was covered with volcanoes and jungles, and
when fierce dinosaurs ruled the earth...

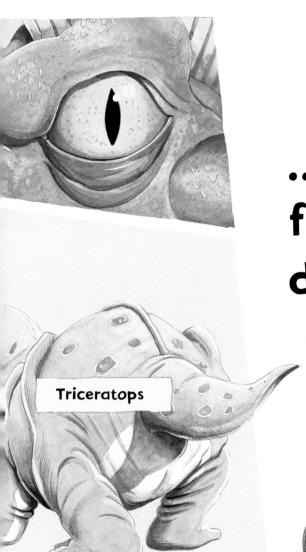

...the fiercest dinosaur of all was...

Triceratops

Tinyrannosaurus
(wrecks).

Because he wasn't as big as some of the other dinosaurs, Tiny had to be especially fierce to make up for it.

ROAR!

So he had learned to **roar** the loudest roar, **clash** his jaws the hardest and pull the **fiercest** faces.

He was the loudest, hardest, fiercest
and grumpiest little dinosaur ever!

He **stamped** and **growled**
and would kick up a storm.
But today Tiny was even grumpier
than normal.

He had an awful toothache, which was not good
news, as everyone knows dinosaurs love to EAT!

"I'm famished," grumbled Tiny, as he sat
down to breakfast. He bit down hard on his
favourite food.

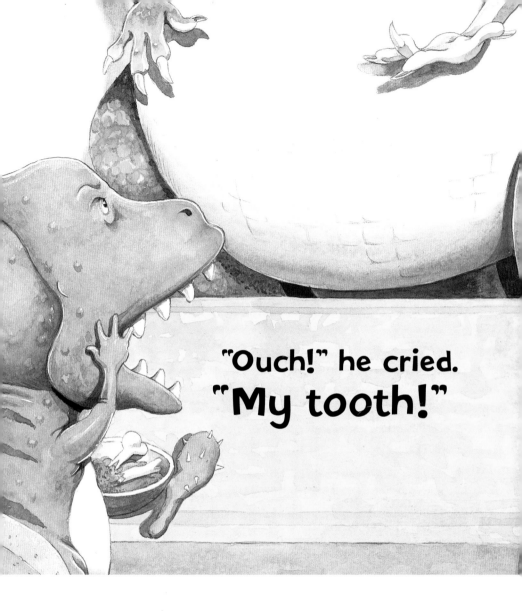

"Ouch!" he cried.
"My tooth!"

"Oh dear," said his mum. "We'd better go
and have that tooth pulled out."

"No way!" cried Tinyrannosaurus,
and off he went to find some friends.

Charge!

Tiny stomped through the jungle in a grumpy mood. His tooth ached and his tummy was empty.

Then, just around the corner, he came upon Triceratops eating in a clearing.

"Food!" smiled Tiny. He roared his loudest
roar. He pulled his fiercest face and bellowed,
"Charge!"

"Careful, Tinyrannosaurus," called Triceratops as Tiny barged into him.

"Yum, yum, yum, yum, OUCH!" Tiny screamed. "My tooth!"

OOOOW!

"Perhaps," said Triceratops,
"you should go and see about having
it removed."

"Not a chance!" sulked Tiny.
"I don't need it out."

Tiny stomped down to the river.
"I'm starving," he moaned, and then he smelt
fresh berries. He followed the scent to a group
of Apatosauruses.

"Charge!" he yelled and stormed towards them, picking up a huge bunch of berries and slamming shut his mighty jaws.

"Ow! Ow! **OUCH!**"
he cried.
"My tooth!"

"Oh dear," said the
Apatosaurus. "Perhaps you
should see about having
it removed."

"I won't have it removed!" sobbed Tiny
and stomped off up the nearest volcano.

He found his best friend, Vilo C Raptor,
who was eating an apple.

"Food!" thundered Tiny, roaring his loudest
roar and pulling his fiercest face.
"Stop, Tiny, STOP!" yelped Vilo.
And as Tiny got within nipping distance of
the apple, he **CLASHED** his mighty jaws.

"YeooOOWWWwwouch!"
howled Tiny.
"What's the matter with
you?" munched Vilo.

"I'm sorry, Vilo," said Tiny, "But I'm so hungry,
and I've got a terrible toothache."
"Then perhaps you'd better go and have it
taken out," said Vilo.

"NO!"
screamed Tiny

"I **WON'T HAVE IT REMOVED!**" and stamping and roaring and growling and grimacing, Tinyrannosaurus kicked up a **REAL STORM**, until the clouds churned and lightning flashed everywhere.

But when the dust settled,
Tiny still had a terrible
toothache and an empty
tummy.
"Oh dear," he sighed.
"Perhaps I had better
have it removed."

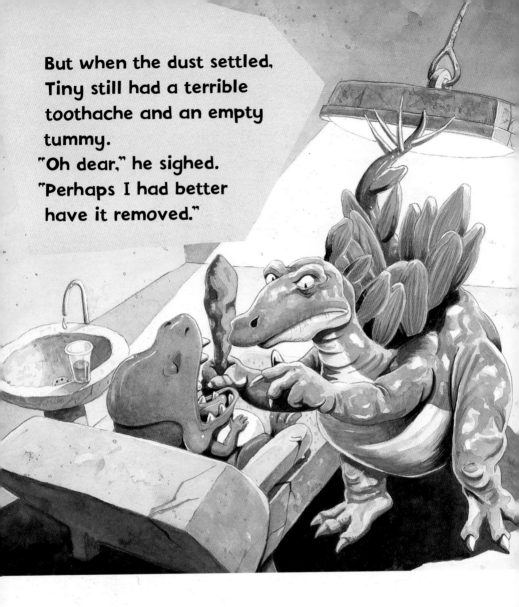

"Open wide," said Dr Stegosaurus peering inside
  Tiny's mouth.
  Tap, tap, tap. "How does that feel?" he asked.
"Much better, thank you," said Tiny.
"Good. You should be able to eat something now,"
  smiled the Dentist.

"I can?!" said Tiny, and jumped up, mouth open, and went

CHOMP!

"Oh Tiny," sighed his mum,
"Please, put the dentist back."

TINY-
RANNOSAURUS
AND THE
NEVERSAURUS

Nick
Ward

Tinyrannosaurus (wrecks) loves his bedtime
stories, and because he is the fiercest little
dinosaur ever, he especially likes **SCARY** stories.
The scarier, the better!
"Tell me a story, Mum," Tiny said when he
was tucked up in bed. "A scary story."

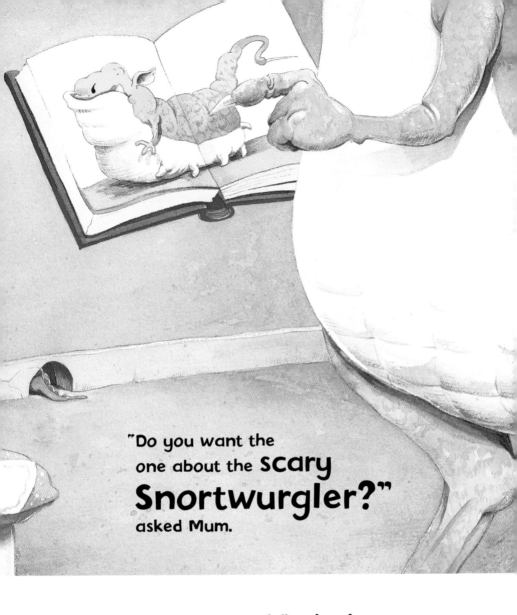

"Do you want the
one about the **scary**
Snortwurgler?"
asked Mum.

"That's not scary enough," said Tiny.
"Then I'll tell you about the ferocious,
fire-breathing Neversaurus," Mum said.
Tiny gulped. He liked that one.

"When the moon is high and the night is dark, the **ferocious, fire-breathing Neversaurus** pads quietly through the streets," said Mum.

"Gnashing his big yellow teeth, the Neversaurus peers through the windows and growls through the locks, making sure all little dinosaurs are safely tucked up in bed.

"Even though no one has ever seen the Neversaurus, you must be very careful,

because if the Neversaurus ever sees a little
dinosaur like you out after dark he..."

But there Mum stopped, because
Tinyrannosaurus was already fast asleep!

Early the next morning, Tiny made some
sandwiches, got out his biggest fishing net
and marched into the garden.
"Where are you going?" asked Mum.

"I'm going to catch
that ferocious, fire-breathing
Neversaurus," said Tiny.

"Well, make sure you are back
in time for tea," smiled Mum.

Tinyrannosaurus
wasn't scared of
anything and he
roared his
loudest roar as
he tiptoed through
the jewel bright
jungle, fishing net
at the ready.

"This is just
the sort of
place to find
a Neversaurus,"
he thought.

Then he heard a noise
coming from the
undergrowth.
A rumbling,
wheezing
noise.

Tiny swung his net. "Got you, you horrible
Neversaurus," he growled.

But...

"Oh Tiny," said Baby Kong. "I was having my nap."
"Sorry I caught you napping," said Tiny.
"But I'm hunting the ferocious, fire-breathing
Neversaurus."

"I'll help," said Baby Kong, and they roared
their loudest roars and pulled their fiercest
faces and went on their way.

"This is just the sort of place to find a
Neversaurus," whispered Tiny as they tiptoed up
to the edge of the bubbling, sulphurous swamp.

"There he is," said Baby Kong, pointing to a large
horn sticking out of the mud.

Tiny swung his net. "Got you, you horrible Neversaurus!" they bellowed.

But...

"Oh Tiny," said Dinoceros. "I was having a wallow."

"Sorry to stop your wallowing," said Tiny.
"But we're after the ferocious, fire-breathing
  Neversaurus."

"I'll help," said Dinoceros, and they roared their loudest roars and crashed their mighty jaws and went off to find the ferocious, fire-breathing Neversaurus.

"We are bound to find the Neversaurus here," said
Tiny, after they had waded through the tall, prickly
prairie grass and climbed to the top of a boulder.

They looked all around. "There he is," cried
Dinoceros. Tiny swung his net.

"**Oh no!** This is ridiculous," yelled Tiny, getting very grumpy indeed. All they had caught was a rather dozy Brontosaurus, munching lazily on the grass.
"We'll never find the Neversaurus at this rate."

"Let's climb the big volcano," suggested Baby Kong. "We'll be able to see for miles and miles from there."

So the three friends marched off to the big volcano. The sun started to set as they looked out over the valley. They couldn't see a Neversaurus anywhere.

"Perhaps we should go home," shivered Baby Kong.

"If the Neversaurus finds us out after dark,
   he'll..."
"I'm not scared of him," said Tinyrannosaurus.
"We've looked everywhere. I **DON'T BELIEVE
THERE IS SUCH A THING AS A SILLY
NEVERSAURUS,**" he shouted.

But if only they could see what you can see!

The ferocious Neversaurus roared his mightiest roar, blowing plumes of smoke and coils of fire into the air.

"Quick," cried the friends.
"The volcano is erupting!"

As the ground shook and the sky filled with flares and flashes and whizz-bangs, they scampered all the way down the hill.

"Good," smiled the Neversaurus. "They should get home in time for tea."

"Did you find your ferocious, fire-breathing
Neversaurus?" asked Mum, when Tiny raced
into the kitchen.

"No," complained Tiny. "We never saw the
Neversaurus, and the Neversaurus never
saw us!"

But we know better, don't we!

TINY-
RANNOSAURUS
AND THE
BIGFOOTOSAURUS

Nick Ward

It was cold and snowy, but Tinyrannosaurus (wrecks) didn't mind. He was the roughest, toughest, fiercest little dinosaur ever.
(He was wearing his warm hat and scarf too!)

He had been tobogganing with his friends all morning, and now they were quite worn out.

"I know," said Tiny. "Let's build a snowman."

So Tinyrannosaurus and his friends built the **biggest** and **meanest** looking snowman you have ever seen, right on top of a tall hill.

"It looks just like a Bigfootosaurus," laughed Tiny. Tinyrannosaurus and his friends danced around the snowman singing, "We're not afraid of the Bigfootosaurus."

Meanwhile, on the other side
of the hill, a **REAL**
Bigfootosaurus was wondering
just who was standing on the
top of his hill.

(It looked like another Bigfoot and he wasn't
having that!)
"My hill," he grunted, and started to march to
the top.

"Silly old Bigfootosaurus," cried Tiny's friends, busy pulling faces at their snowman.

"My hill," Bigfootosaurus grunted again, and with one swipe of his mighty paw, he squashed the snowman flat!

And, oh dear, Tiny and his friends were so busy laughing that they didn't notice that their snowman had changed.

"A Bigfootosaurus couldn't
scare me," said Baby Kong.
"If I met a real Bigfootosaurus,
I would pull his tail.

Like this!"

The Bigfootosaurus grumbled.

"And if I met a real Bigfootosaurus, I would
snowball him just like this," cried Dinoceros.
The Bigfootosaurus growled.

"If I met a real Bigfootosaurus, I would scare him to pieces with my terrific roar!" bellowed Tiny. **"Grrrnash!"**

Grrrnash!

Tiny's friends laughed.

The Bigfootosaurus raised his hairy arms and flexed his sharp claws.
"Oh yeah?" he bellowed.

"Rarrr!"

He raced after them, his big monster feet making
the ground rumble and shake!
"Help, run!" shrieked Tiny to his gang.
"OUR SNOWMAN HAS COME TO LIFE!"

Bigfootosaurus was right behind them.
He lifted his big, hairy foot, high above
their heads.
"Rarr!" he roared.

Then he brought his foot crashing down.

"Watch out!" cried Tiny.
But the big monster foot landed on Baby Kong's
toboggan by mistake.

He went skating past Tiny's friends at
top speed.
"Help," he cried. "I can't stop!"
Good, thought Tiny. That will teach him
a lesson.

The Bigfootosaurus was skating straight towards
a deep and dangerous ravine. "Help!" he roared.
He was really, really scared.

"Oh no, our poor snowman,"
cried Tinyrannosaurus.

Tiny and his friends watched their snowman
as he skated closer and closer to the edge
of the ravine.
"What shall we do?" Tiny and his friends chased
after him, but he was going much too fast.

Then Tiny had a brilliant idea!

Tinyrannosaurus
roared his
loudest roar.

"ROAR!"

It was so loud it shook the snow right out of
a big fir tree. It was so loud it shook the snow
right off of the mountainside.

The snow landed in a big heap on the ground.

PLOP! Bigfootosaurus crashed into the big mound of snow and disappeared inside. Everything went very quiet.

"Are you all right, snowman?" asked Tinyrannosaurus, creeping nervously up to the pile of snow.

POP! Bigfootosaurus stuck his head out of the top.

"Oh dear! That's not our snowman,"
cried Tiny. "That's a real Bigfootosaurus.
EVERYBODY RUN!"

"STOP!"

bellowed the Bigfootosaurus.

Everybody stopped.

"You saved me. Thank you. That was some MIGHTY roar!"

Tinyrannosaurus was so pleased and so
proud, he roared again. A terrific roar!
An earth shaking roar!

"No, Tiny!" cried his friends, but it was
too late...

THE
END!

meadowside
CHILDREN'S BOOKS